# Do-It-Yourself Coffins

## For Pets and People

## Dale Power
Text written with & photography by Jeffrey B. Snyder

Schiffer Publishing Ltd

4880 Lower Valley Road, Atglen, PA 19310 USA

# Acknowledgments

I would like to thank the people who helped with this book. Peter Zietzke and his son Ben, and Jeff Snyder who made this a fun book to do. I would also like to thank my friends at Delta and Woodcrafters.

Happy woodworking!

— Dale Power Sr.

Copyright © 1997 by Dale L. Power
Library of Congress Catalog Card Number: 97-67262

Designed by Laurie A. Smucker
ISBN: 978-0-7643-0337-1
Printed in China

Published by Schiffer Publishing, Ltd.
4880 Lower Valley Road
Atglen, PA 19310
Phone: (610) 593-1777; Fax: (610) 593-2002
E-mail: Info@schifferbooks.com
Web: www.schifferbooks.com

For our complete selection of fine books on this and related subjects, please visit our website at www.schifferbooks.com. You may also write for a free catalog.

Schiffer Publishing's titles are available at special discounts for bulk purchases for sales promotions or premiums. Special editions, including personalized covers, corporate imprints, and excerpts, can be created in large quantities for special needs. For more information, contact the publisher.

We are always looking for people to write books on new and related subjects. If you have an idea for a book, please contact us at proposals@schifferbooks.com.

# Table of Contents

# Introduction

For years I have been interested in coffins — their history, construction, and traditions. I hope to give everyone a chance to explore these fascinating objects around which so much history, ceremony, and emotion revolves. It will also be interesting to consider the options, some coffin designs may also be useful and beautiful pieces of furniture.

Coffin making has always been a grave matter; throughout time people have used boxes of one sort or another to contain the bodies of their loved ones for their eternal sleep. Coffins have had many names: sarcophagus, casket, coffin, and the old pine box.

Let's face it, coffin is also a word that some people are very uncomfortable with. In this book we will show you that if you give it another name, you can think of this particularly well crafted and sturdy box in other ways. You will be surprised at the number of uses you will come up with for the boxes you make — uses far different from those for which you will finally need them.

Look at the furnishings around your home, if you examine the shapes you will see that almost everything looks like a box. A bookcase is only a box standing up with boards to hold your printed treasures. Why not have a coffee table to store extra blankets and pillows?

In this book we will explore many of the techniques available to make coffins for you, your loved-ones, and your pets.

## Materials and Tools

Detailed plans for each of the six coffin projects have been provided. Be sure to refer to them often while working through the individual construction steps of each coffin. The wood used for these projects includes pine and poplar boards and cabinet grade birch plywood. Woodworking tools required to complete these projects include: a 12" planer, safety glasses, a table saw, dado blades to be used on the table saw, a jointer, a biscuit cutter, biscuits, Titebond or Gorilla Glue, yellow carpenter's glue, strap clamps, a screwdriver and 1 1/4" sheet rock screws, a power sander and sand paper of varying grits, a power drill with assorted bits, wooden dowels, a hammer and nails, a hand held saw, a staple gun, wood molding in designs which suit your taste in coffin finishes, and satin lining material and batting.

Exterior and interior finishes include Minwax stain and sealer in red mahogany and black walnut. I also used a Minwax wood stain rubbing oil in rosewood color. Quick finishes are applied with Formby's textured stone spray paint. For the application of stains, wear rubber gloves. You will also find a sponge and a 1 1/2" synthetic brush useful.

# Coffin Pattern Charts

| PINE COFFIN (Drawings A1& A2) | | | | | | | |
|---|---|---|---|---|---|---|---|
| Coffin Size | Length Size A | Bisect Angle A, B &F | Length B & F | Bisect Angle B&C,E&F | Length C & E | Bisect Angle C,E & D | Length D |
| 5'-8" | 12" | 35.5º | 19 1/8" | 11.25º | 50-1/8" | 43.25º | 18" |
| 6'-0" | 12" | 35.5º | 19 1/8" | 11.1º | 54-18" | 43.4º | 18" |
| 6'-3" | 12" | 35.5º | 19 1/8" | 11.0º | 57 1/8" | 43.5º | 18" |

| PINE COFFIN LID (Drawings A1 & A2 ) | | | | | | | |
|---|---|---|---|---|---|---|---|
| Coffin Size | Length Size a1 | Bisect Angle a1,b1,c1 | Length b1,f1 | Bisect Angle b1,c1,e1,f1 | Length c1,e1 | Bisect Angle c1,e1,d1 | Length d1 |
| 5'-8" | 12" | 35.5º | 19 1/8" | 11.25º | 50-1/8" | 43.25º | 18" |
| 6'-0" | 12" | 35.5º | 19 1/8" | 11.1º | 54-18" | 43.4º | 18" |
| 6'-3" | 12" | 35.5º | 19 1/8" | 11.0º | 57 1/8" | 43.5º | 18" |

| PLYWOOD COFFIN (Drawings B1 & B2) | | | | | | | |
|---|---|---|---|---|---|---|---|
| Coffin Size | Length Size A | Bisect Angle A, B &F | Length B & F | Bisect Angle B&C,E&F | Length C & E | Bisect Angle C,E & D | Length D |
| 5'-8" | 12" | 25.5º | 19 1/8" | 11.25º | 50-1/8" | 45º | 24" |
| 6'-0" | 12" | 25.5º | 19 1/8" | 11.1º | 54-18" | 45º | 24" |
| 6'-3" | 12" | 25.5º | 19 1/8" | 11.0º | 57 1/8" | 45º | 24" |

| PLYWOOD COFFIN (Drawings B1 & B2) | | | | | | | |
|---|---|---|---|---|---|---|---|
| Coffin Size | Length Size a1 | Bisect Angle a1,b1,c1 | Length b1,f1 | Bisect Angle b1,c1,e1,f1 | Length c1,e1 | Bisect Angle c1,e1,d1 | Length d1 |
| 5'-8" | 13" | 25.5º | 20 1/8" | 11.25º | 51-1/8" | 45º | 25" |
| 6'-0" | 13" | 25.5º | 20 1/8" | 11.1º | 55-18" | 45º | 25" |
| 6'-3" | 13" | 25.5º | 20 1/8" | 11.0º | 58 1/8" | 45º | 25" |

| POPLAR COFFIN (Drawings C1 & C2 ) | | | | | |
|---|---|---|---|---|---|
| Coffin Siz Size | Length A, C | Bisect Angle A,B | Length B & D | Bisect Angle B&C | Bisect Angl C & D |
| 5'-8" | 24" | 90º | 5'-8" | 90º | 45º |
| 6'-0" | 24" | 90º | 6'-0" | 90º | 45º |
| 6'-3" | 24" | 90º | 6'-3" | 90º | 45º |

| POPLAR COFFIN LID (Drawings C1 & C2 ) | | | | | |
|---|---|---|---|---|---|
| Coffin Siz Size | Length a1&c1 | Bisect Angle a1,b1 | Length b1&d1 | Bisect Angle b1,c1 | Bisect Angl c1,d1 |
| 5'-8" | 24" | 45º | 5'-8" | 45º | 45º |
| 6'-0" | 24" | 45º | 6'-0" | 45º | 45º |
| 6'-3" | 24" | 45º | 6'-3" | 45º | 45º |
| | a2&c2 | | b2 &d2 | | |
| 5'-8" | 23" | SEE DRAWING | 5'-7" | SEE DRAWING | |
| 6,-0" | 23" | SEE DRAWING | 5'-11" | SEE DRAWING | |
| 6'-3" | 23" | SEE DRAWING | 6'-2" | SEE DRAWING | |

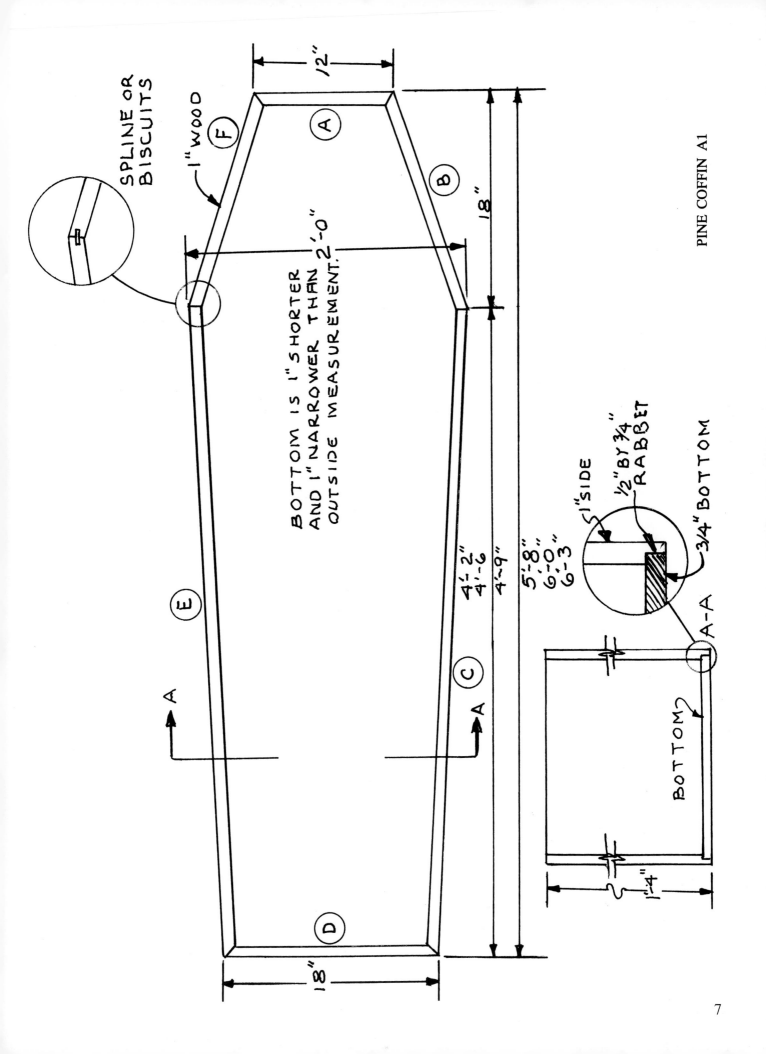

SPLINE OR BISCUITS

1" WOOD

12"

18"

BOTTOM IS 1" SHORTER AND 1" NARROWER THAN OUTSIDE MEASUREMENT. 2'-0"

4'-2"
4'-6"
4'-9"
5'-8"
6'-0"
6'-3"

1" SIDE

½" BY ¾" RABBET

¾" BOTTOM

A-A

BOTTOM

1'-4"

18"

PINE COFFIN A1

7

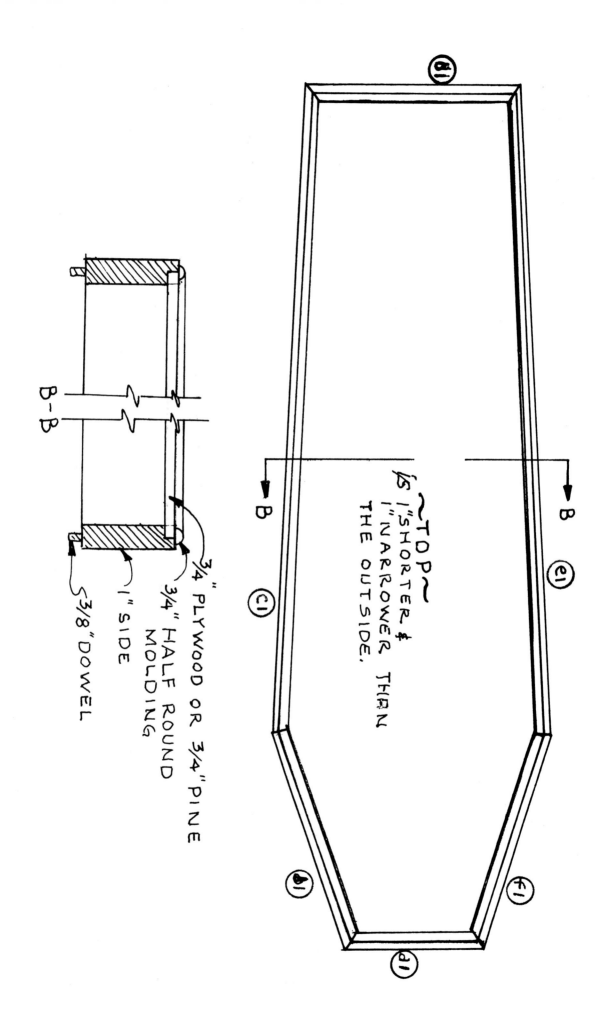

~TOP~
is 1"SHORTER &
1"NARROWER THAN
THE OUTSIDE.

B - B

3/4" PLYWOOD OR 3/4" PINE

3/4" HALF ROUND
MOLDING

1" SIDE

3/8" DOWEL

B

PINE COFFIN A2

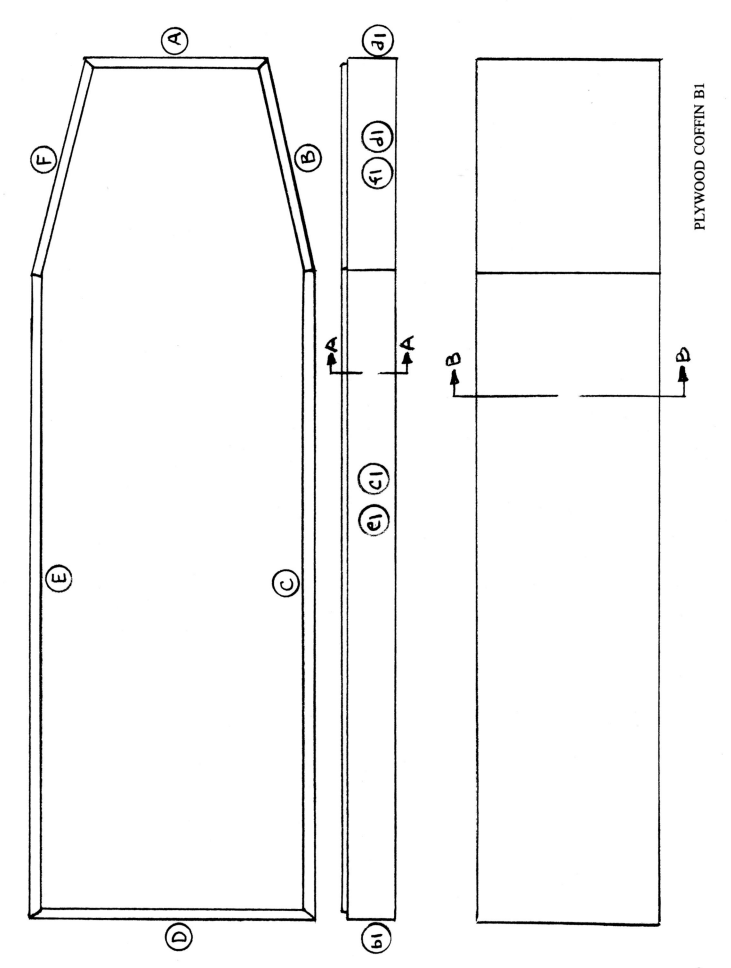

PLYWOOD COFFIN B1

9

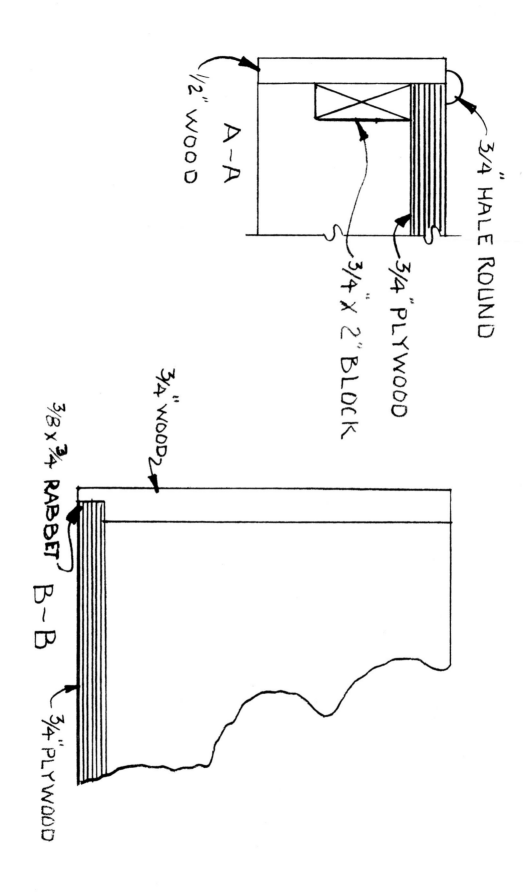

A-A

1/2" WOOD

3/4" HALF ROUND

3/4" PLYWOOD

3/4" x 2" BLOCK

3/4" WOOD

3/8 x 3/4 RABBET

B-B

3/4" PLYWOOD

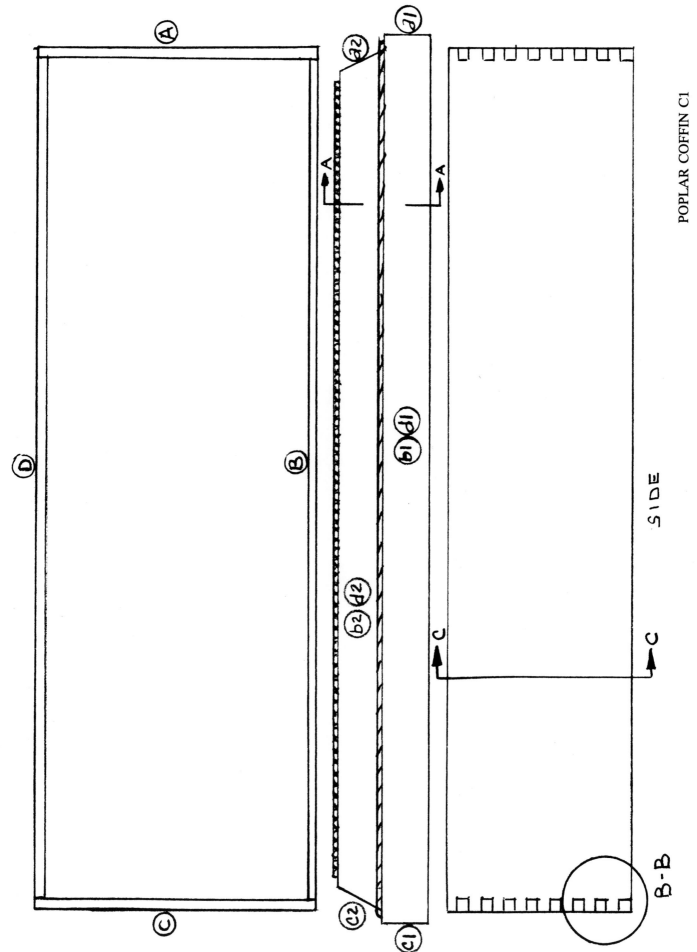

POPLAR COFFIN C1

SIDE

B-B

11

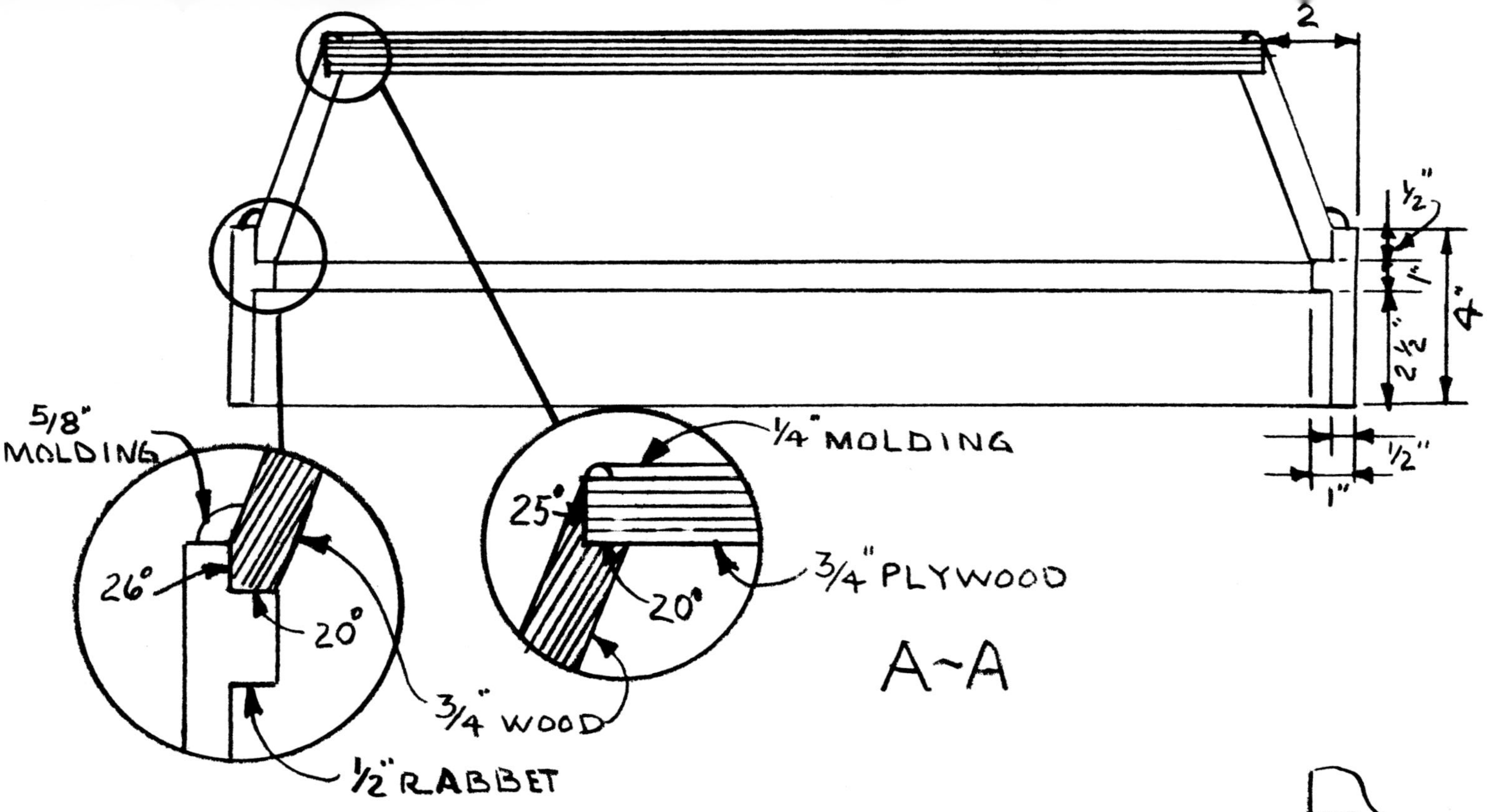

16"

24"

3/4" PLYWOOD

3/4"
PLYWOOD

1/2" x 3/4" RABBET

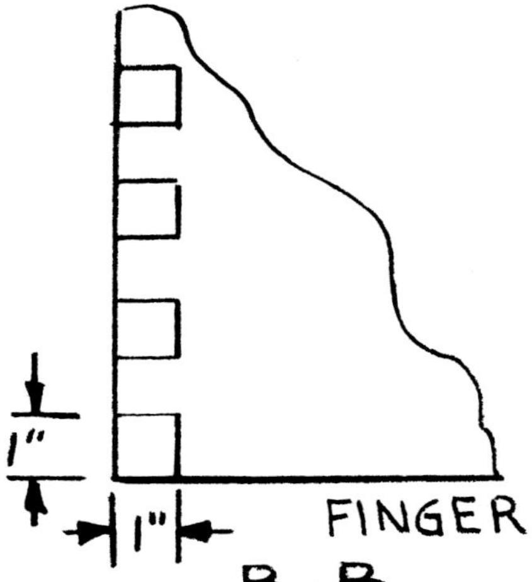

1" WOOD

5/8"
MOLDING

26°

20°

1/2" RABBET

3/4" WOOD

A~A

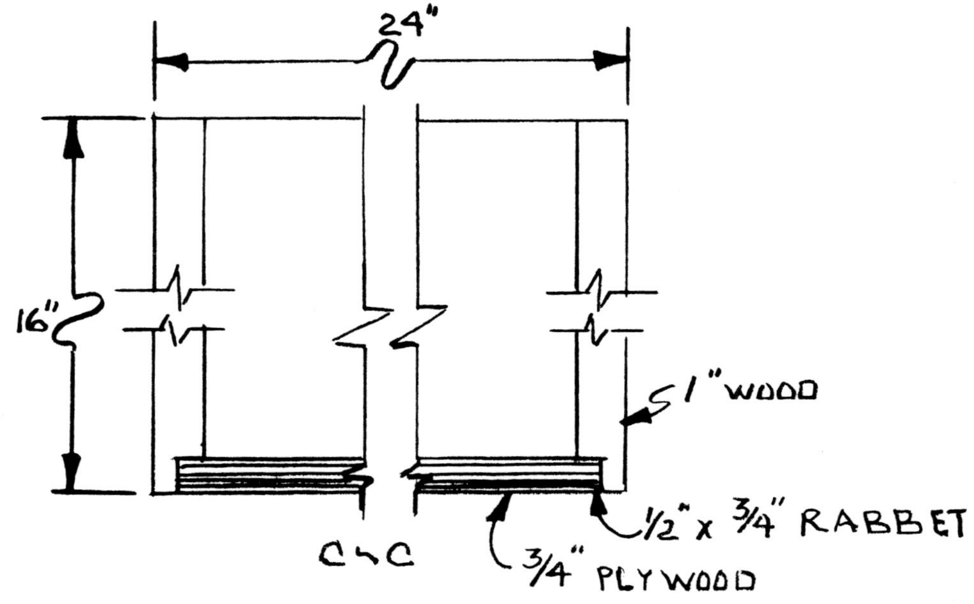

25°

20°

3/4" PLYWOOD

1/4" MOLDING

2

1"

1/2"

2 1/2"

1"

1/2"

4"

1"

1"

B~B

FINGER JOINTS

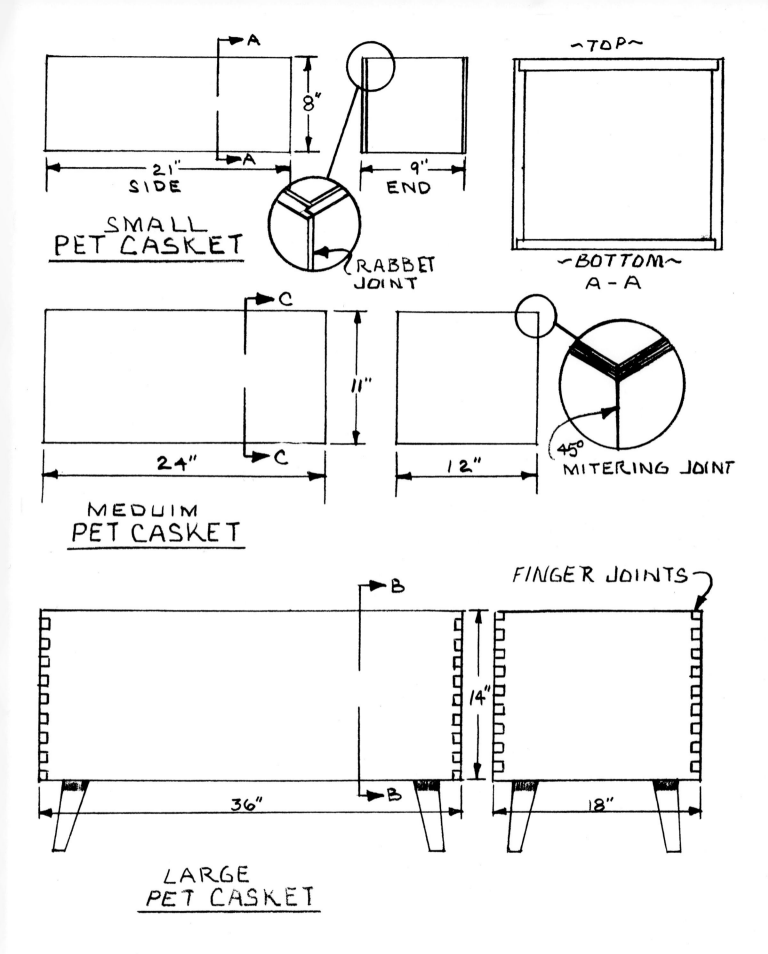

## SMALL PET CASKET

8"

21"
SIDE

9"
END

RABBET JOINT

~TOP~

~BOTTOM~
A – A

## MEDUIM PET CASKET

24"

11"

12"

45°
MITERING JOINT

## LARGE PET CASKET

FINGER JOINTS

14"

36"

18"

LARGE, MEDIUM, AND SMALL PET COFFINS D1

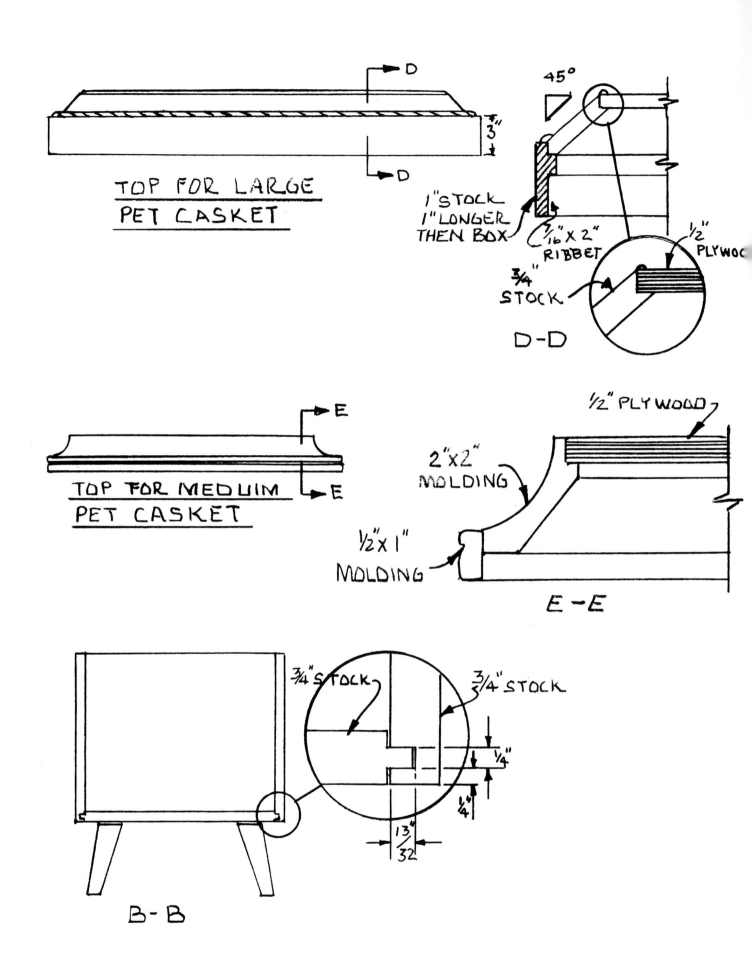

TOP FOR LARGE PET CASKET

45°

1" STOCK 1" LONGER THEN BOX

$\frac{1}{16}$" X 2" RIBBET

$\frac{3}{4}$" STOCK

$\frac{1}{2}$" PLYWOO

D-D

3"

TOP FOR MEDUIM PET CASKET

$\frac{1}{2}$" PLYWOOD

2" X 2" MOLDING

$\frac{1}{2}$" X 1" MOLDING

E-E

$\frac{3}{4}$" STOCK

$\frac{3}{4}$" STOCK

$\frac{1}{4}$"

$\frac{1}{4}$"

$\frac{13}{32}$"

B-B

LARGE, MEDIUM, AND SMALL PET COFFINS D2

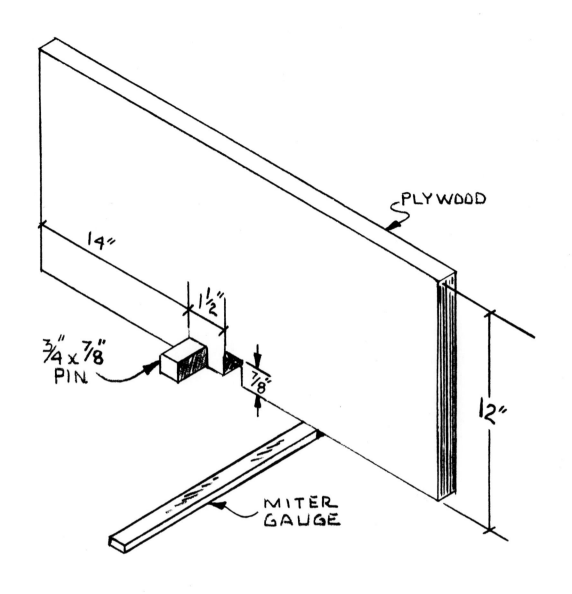

PLYWOOD

14"

1½"

3/4" x 7/8" PIN

7/8"

MITER GAUGE

12"

## MAKE A FINGER JOINT JIG

START BY SECURING A 12" X 24" PIECE OF PLYWOOD TO YOUR MITER GAUGE AND CUT A 3/4" X 7/8" DADO. GLUE OR SCREW A GUIDE PIN IN THE DADO. THEN RESECURE THE FENCE EXACTLY 1½" OVER TOWARD THE RIP FINCE, OR PUT ANOTHER PRICE OF 3/4" PLYWOOD BETWEEN THE PIN AND THE DADO HEAD.

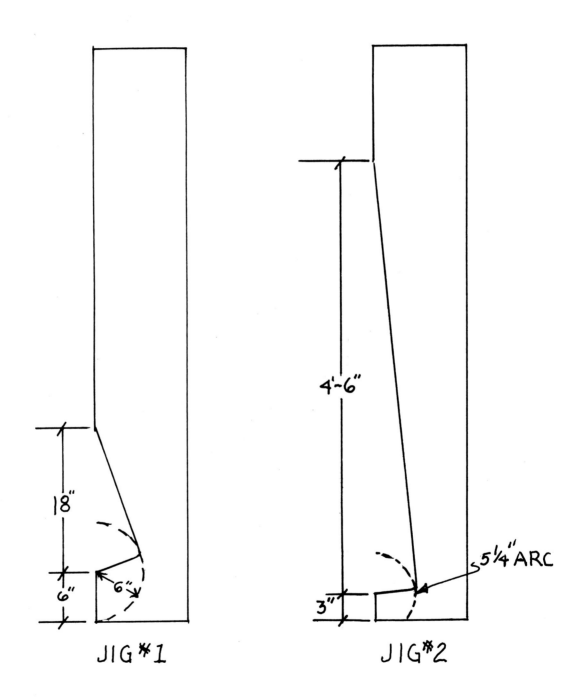

JIG #1

JIG #2

COFFIN LID

# Six Coffin Projects

Using a 12" Delta planer, plane the surfaces all of the wood to be used on each coffin project. All of your boards should be a uniform 3/4" thick.

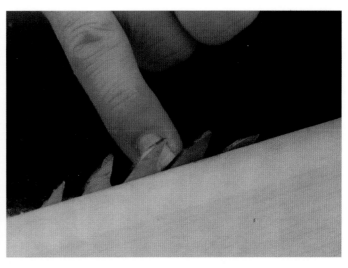

Always set the blade so that the valley of the highest tooth is just visible over the surface of the wood. This technique exposes as little blade as possible when cutting.

For your own safety, always read the instructions prior to operating your power tools. Always remember to wear safety glasses or safety goggles when operating power tools.

Square up the edges of the wood with the saw blade.

Never depend on the accuracy of the scale on the table saw when setting the blade angle; always check the angle of the blade set that you want with a tri-square. Note: the saw guard has been removed only for the clarity of the photographs. Never operate this, or any other power tool, without the safety guards in place.

Always use some type of pushing device when feeding wood through the saw. Run every board through the saw to ensure that they are all the same width (refer to the coffin patterns for widths).

# The first coffin for people

The first coffin we will make is the classic pine box (refer to the PINE COFFIN patterns). The first step is to create a template to follow while cutting the angled top and bottom of the pine coffin. Shown here is the template for the head end of the coffin. The angle of the template is set at 90 degrees to the end of the board.

Use a scrap piece of wood to make a jig. This jig will be used when cutting the top and bottom coffin pieces. Begin laying out the jig by measuring 6" up from the bottom of the scrap board and marking this point. Next, take a compass and strike a 6" arc. Measure 18" more from the 6" mark. Draw an angled line from the 18" point along the leading edge of the board back and up to the upper outside edge of the 6" arc. Draw a second angled line from the point where the first line intersects the 6" arc back to the 6" point along the leading edge of the board. When done correctly, this should create a 90 degrees angle.

Cut along the pencil lines.

Fit a board into the jig to make the top corner of the coffin lid. This step will be repeated on 4 boards to make the angle for top and bottom boards of the pine coffin. This creates the angled lid and base of the coffin above the coffin's "shoulder."

Following the same procedures, create a second jig from a length of scrap wood. This will be the jig for the second cut on both sides of the top and bottom boards, the cuts which will create the angle for the lid and base below the coffin's "shoulder" (refer to the pint coffin patterns) To make the second jig, measure up 3" from the bottom of the board and mark a point. From that new point, measure 4' 6" further up the board. Once both points are marked, go back to the 3" point and swing a 5 1/4" arc with your compass. Draw a line from the 4' 6" measurement point along the outside edge of the board up to the top outside point along the 5 1/4" arc. Connect a second line from the point on the arc you have just established back to the original 3" mark. This makes an long, angled 90 degree corner.

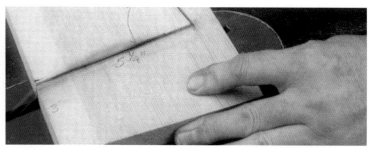

Cutting the first angle of the jig along the marked line.

Cutting the second angle of the jig along the marked line.

Cutting the long angle for the lid and base using the second jig.

It is time to cut all the remaining coffin boards (the boards which make up the coffin walls) to length. Refer to the chart for lengths and angles of cut. Be sure to mark your pieces A, B, C, and so on in order of placement around the coffin. Use these letter marks only on the side of each board that will be facing into the coffin. In this shot I am cutting A (the head board) to length. Always cut your angles with the inside of the boards to the saw table. Once you have set an angle, cut the corresponding angles on opposite boards such as the connecting cuts on boards B and F (the angles which connect to A - the head board).

Cut the angles on head board A as shown in the chart. Refer to the chart to be sure of your angles.

Cut sections B & F to the same length. (For purposes of illustration, I have marked the outside of each board with its letter designation. Don't follow this example or you will have to spend extra time later cleaning the outside of your pine coffin before you can stain it.)

Cut sections C & E to the same length.

Cut the length for section D.

The identical angle has been cut on the other side of head board A.

The first angle to be cut on board B is the same as the angle on board A. This is the adjoining angle for A & B. To save yourself some time, once an angle is set, use it to cut the angle for all adjoining boards. In this case, B and F (the same board above the "shoulder" on opposite sides of the coffin) have adjoining angles with head board A.

Now make the second cuts on boards C and E, the steeper angles which adjoin with board D (the foot of the coffin).

The second angle cut on board B is much shallower. The second cut creates the adjoining angles for boards B and C. Repeat this cut on board F, board B's counterpart on the other side of the coffin.

Leave the blade at the same angle and cut the angles on board D.

After cutting the second angle on boards B and F, we are ready to cut the first angles on boards C and E.

The angle cut on board D.

It is time to fasten both halves of the coffin lid together with biscuits and glue. First line up both halves of the coffin lid. Next, from the top of the coffin lid, measure down 2" and put a pencil mark across both boards. Every 6" below that 2" mark, put marks across both boards. This will allow us to align a biscuit cutter on each half of the lid while cutting the slots needed to hold the biscuits. The biscuits and glue will secure both halves of the lid.

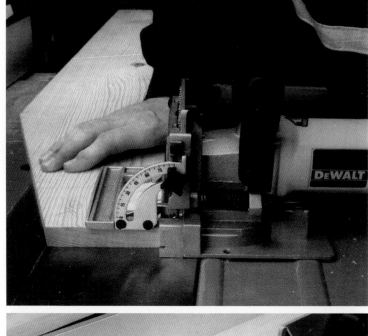

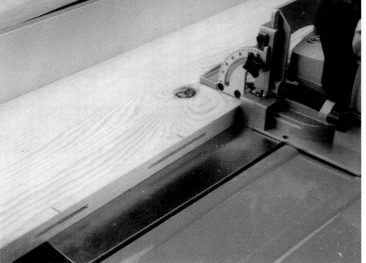

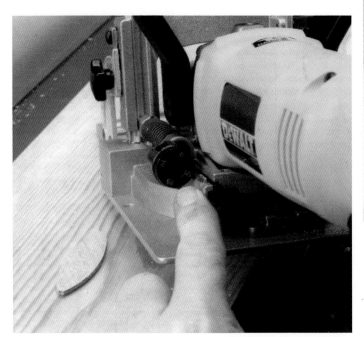

Set the depth gauge at 10 on the biscuit cutter. By doing this, the slot cut will accommodate the size 10 biscuit shown here.

Cutting biscuit slots with the biscuit cutter. If you have never used a biscuit cutter before, it has a witness mark (usually in red) to indicate the center of the biscuit cutter. Align this center mark with the pencil mark on the lid. Also check you depth gauge to make sure the setting is correct. Cut in the biscuit slots.

On the second half of the lid, make sure you have the same face up as you did on the previous board. This guarantees that the cuts will match. I mark my boards to indicate which side of each board is the inside.

To secure the biscuits, you may either use Titebond wood glue or a new type of glue called Gorilla Glue. Gorilla Glue goes on dark and dries to a natural color. If your wood is wet or you wish to fill irregularities, the Gorilla Glue is water activated and swells to fill gaps. If your wood is dry, a little dab of water will activate the Gorilla Glue.

Run the boards through the jointer to straighten the top and bottom edges prior to putting the biscuits in place and gluing them.

Dampening the slots prior to using Gorilla Glue and inserting the biscuits.

Apply Gorilla Glue along the centerline and into the biscuit slots on one half of the lid and into the slots only on the other half of the lid.

Cut all 6 pieces to length.

Insert the biscuits into the slots on one half of the lid, join both halves of the lid, and clamp the joined halves together tightly until dried. If you are using cloth clamps, place a few biscuits under the clamp straps near the glued joint to prevent the clamps from being glued to the boards. Repeat this process for the bottom of the coffin as well. Clamp both top and bottom sections and set them aside to dry. Remember, the curing time on this glue is from 1 to 4 hours depending on the temperature, humidity, and water content of the glue.

We are set up to cut the bands which make up the vertical sides of the coffin lid. Mark all of your bands inside as you cut them. This will keep them properly oriented for further cutting. Mark these boards a1 through e1.

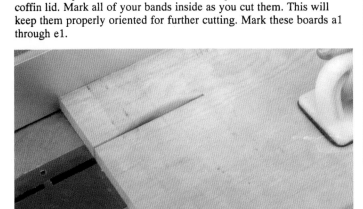

Remember to cut the angles from the inside out, meaning that the inside of each coffin part is down to the face of the table during cutting.

Begin by cutting the angle on a1. Repeat this procedure on all other edge pieces, cutting all corresponding angles.

We want to cut a dado 3/4" width x 3/8" depth in the bottom of the coffin body wall sections A, B, C, D, E, and F.  In time, the coffin base will fit into this dado and secured.

With the same dado head setting for width and depth, we are going to cut a dado in the top of a1, b1, c1, d1, e1, and f1 to receive the flat top of the coffin lid. Remember to place the inside down toward the table top.

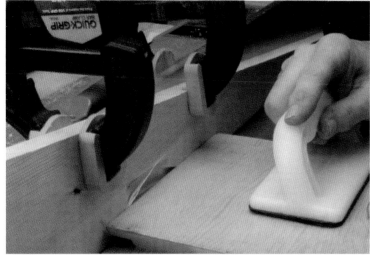

The dado has been cut into the inside top edge of a1. Repeat this cut on b1 through f1.

Set the dado head blades (refer to the instructions that accompany the blades) to cut a 3/4" width, 3/8" depth dado. Cutting the dado into the base of one wall section.

Using the procedure described before, cut Number 10 biscuit slots into all of the angles on A, B, C, D, E, and F, the boards which comprise the coffin body.

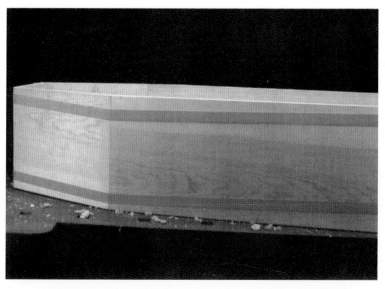

Now we are ready to begin assembling our first coffin, that classic pine box. Dry fit your coffin body together to make sure that all of the joints line up. This job is easier when you use the cloth clamps for support.

Make sure that the screws angle out a bit so that they go into both the dado lip the bottom rests in and the side wall of the coffin itself. This gives the screws extra strength. The screws may be countersunk and filled in later if desired.

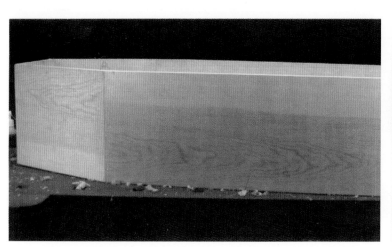

Glue the coffin sides together and set them aside. Once the body is dried, remove the bands and attach the bottom.

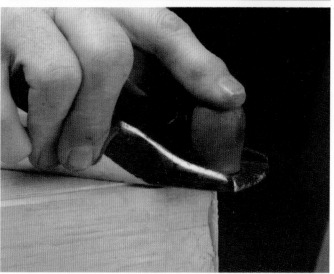

The coffin bottom is attached with yellow carpenter's glue and 1 1/4" sheet rock screws. Here I am applying the carpenter's glue.

Check all of the coffin corners to make sure that they are level. If they are not, you can reduce them with a small hand plane.

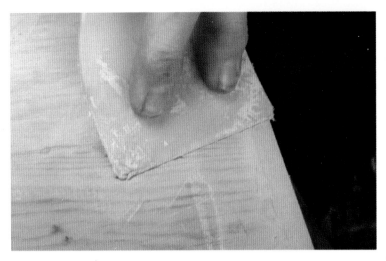

This is a good time to fill in any nicks, holes, or seams you deem necessary on both the top and the bottom of the coffin. I am using carpenter's wood filler.

Fill in the joint between the two halves of the bottom and along the joints between the sidewalls and the base.

With 80 grit sandpaper, begin sanding the coffin lid smooth.

Here is a trick to ensure uniform sanding and a level surface across the coffin lid and base. Begin by marking pencil lines across your center joint. When the pencil marks are sanded away from both sides of the joint, the area on both sides of the joint is level.

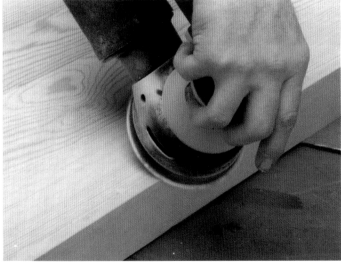

Lightly sand all of the exposed edges and corners to prevent denting or chipping.

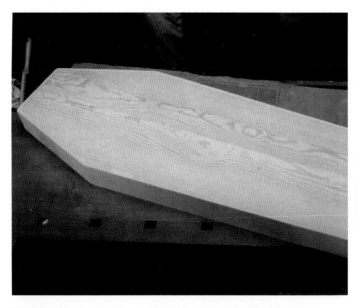

The lid has been sanded smooth. Its corners and edges have been rounded.

To orient the dowels properly so that the top will align itself with the body, I have made a jig out of scrap wood. The overall length of this jig is 6" x 7/8". It is divided down the center with a line. Working from one end, measure in 1 1/2" and place a mark perpendicular to the center line. Measure another 1 1/2" and place a second mark perpendicular to the center line. Repeat this process until you have four lines measured in, each 1 1/2" from the mark before it.

Sand off any extraneous markings on the outside of the box. Round all of the edges and corners to reduce the chance of damage.

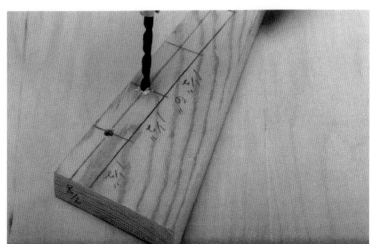

Using a 3/16" bit, drill holes at each measured junction along the jig. Make sure to drill the holes all the way through.

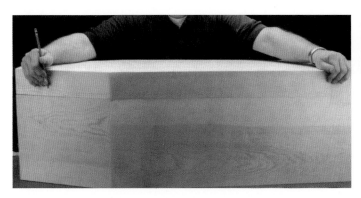

Evenly space two witness marks on either side of the coffin near the head and foot. These four witness marks (lightly drawn on both the coffin body and lid) will be used to locate the dowels which will help align the lid to the body of the coffin.

After the holes are drilled, cut your jig out, insert short pieces of dowel into the holes, and draw the center line of the center hole out over one of the edges.

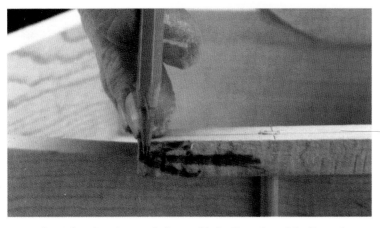

A word to the wise: mark the outside leading edge of the jig so that you will use it the same way every time. If you do not use the jig the same way each time, the holes in the body and lid will not match up later.

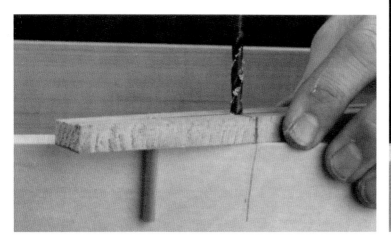

Set the jig in place with a dowel on either side of the side wall. Align the center line mark with the witness lines on the outside of the coffin. Drill straight down into the center hole of the jig. Repeat this process at all four witness marks.

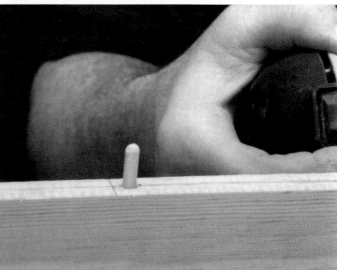

Cut four dowels to equal lengths and round the outer ends prior to fitting the dowels into the lid. Test the dowels in the drilled holes prior to gluing them into place.

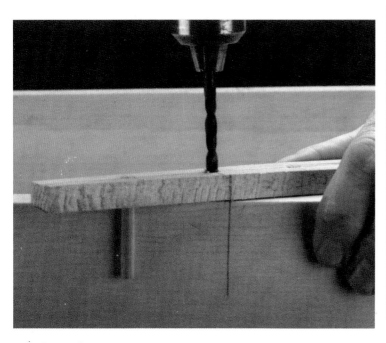

Repeat this process on the coffin lid.

Here is an alternate method for aligning the holes for the dowels. First, mark your drill bit with a piece of tape so that all of the holes will be of the same depth.

Next, insert nails (heads down) into the holes.

Taper the end of the dowel that will be exposed so that it fits in the hole more smoothly and firmly when the lid is lowered.

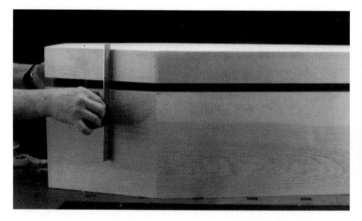

Make sure the top is aligned with the bottom. Tap gently on the lid and the nails will mark where the holes in the lid need to be drilled.

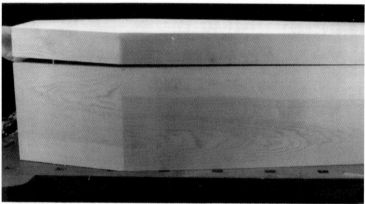

Dry fit the lid before gluing the dowels in place. The lid should fit securely.

Drill at the nail hole marks to the depth marked on the bit.

The lid fits securely.

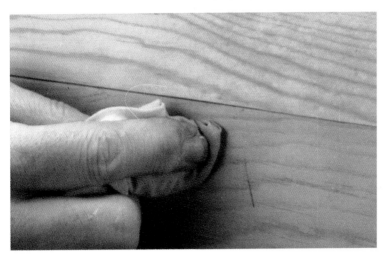

To remove pencil lines from the coffin exterior, use rubbing alcohol and a soft cloth.

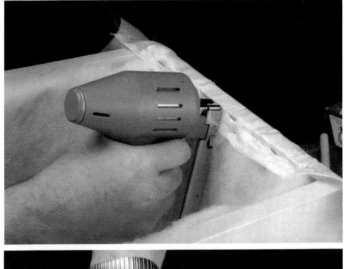

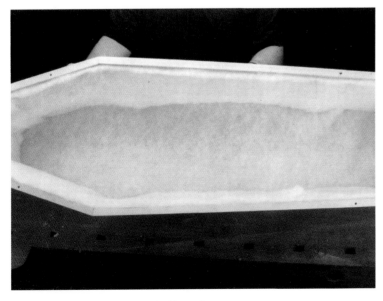

To line the inside of the coffin, first roll out cotton batting along the bottom, then along each side wall. Staple the batting into place with a staple gun.

To secure the satin lining material covering the batting, staple from the inside and then lay the rest of the material down over the staples. Staple near the top of the board but from the inside of the material. This way the staples will be covered when the cloth is folded over into the coffin.

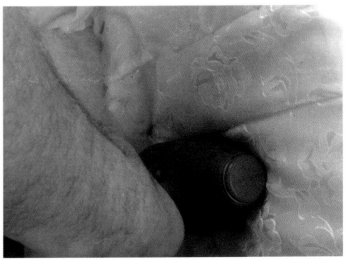

The cotton batting is stapled into place.

It does not matter if the staples show along the bottom of the side walls. The material on the bottom of the coffin will cover this.

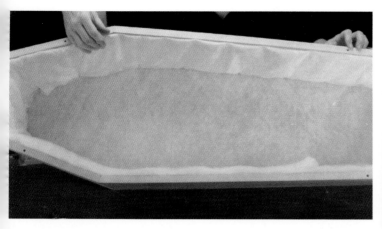

Half of the lining is now in place.

Continue by laying in the material and stapling it along the edge so the folds can be brought back out and the staples won't show. To finish off the head end of the coffin, manufacture a small pillow with batting and the same material used to finish the inside of the coffin. Light sewing is required here.

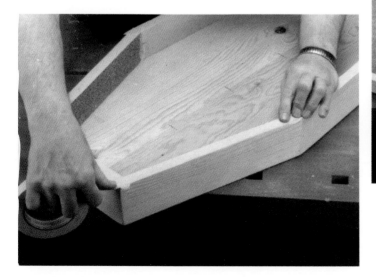

Tape off the leading edges of the lid prior to finishing off the inside of the lid.

For a different look, finish the inside of the lid with textured stone finish spray. Use two coats of spray to give the inside a finished look. Hold the can 10" to 12" from the surface when spraying.

The inside of the lid is finished and the masking tape has been removed from the outer edges.

It is time to stain our first, finished coffin. Begin by masking off the top edge of the coffin body prior to staining. This keeps the stain from getting up on the edge, which would be glued shut upon use. Carefully align the tape with the outside edge of the box. The truer your line, the more accurate your edge will be.

Staining the coffin lid.

I am using a dark walnut Minwax stain and sealer to coat the coffin. Apply the stain with a sponge. Be sure to wear rubber gloves when applying stains. The stain has been applied half way down the outside of the coffin.

The lid is stained. Once the coffin is dry, use a 1 1/2" synthetic brush to apply a finishing coat of polyurethane varnish to the entire coffin.

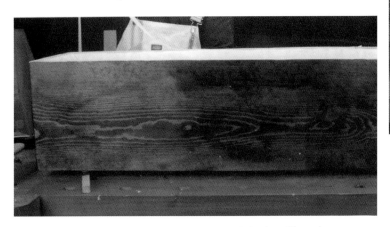

Carefully remove the tape and set the coffin body aside to dry.

# The second coffin for people.

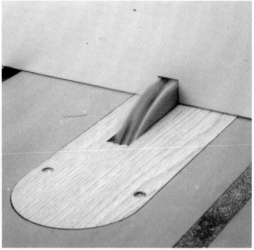

The second coffin is a rectangular, poplar coffin held together using finger joints (refer to POPLAR COFFIN patterns). Because of its shape, legs may be added to this box and it can double as a blanket chest ... until needed. To set up a jig to cut finger joints, take a piece of scrap wood, run it through a 3/4" dado, using the miter guide to support the scrap wood from behind. Cut a dado into the scrap wood as shown.

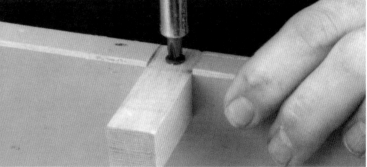

Install a wood block into the cut that is the same size as the miter cut. This block will act as an index pin. The block measures 3/4" x 3/4" x 1 1/2" long. Pre-drill a hole in the bottom of the index pin and the board so as not to split them. Fasten with a screw, making sure the screw is tight enough not to catch on the miter bench.

Take a piece of stock of the width we are going to be running, place it alongside the dado head, and move the index pin up tight against it to achieve the proper spacing. Fasten the index pin and scrap wood to the miter gauge with 2 wood screws.

Run a sample joint through the dado to see if it is properly set or if minor adjustments are needed.

To cut the adjacent corner, move the first piece with the last dado cut over the finger, slide the second piece up against the first and make a cut.

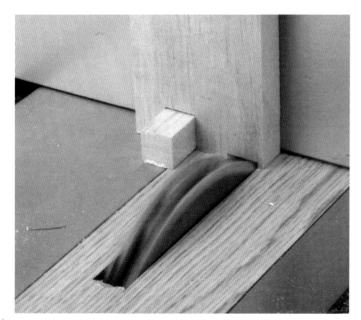

Move the first joint over the index pin and cut your next joint. With this guide, the joints will be evenly spaced.

Remove the first piece, slide the second piece over the index pin and continue.

Using scrap wood, test to see if the finger joints are too large to interlock with each other well. If the joint is too large, the fingers will break. To remedy the situation, readjust the index pin away from the blade by 1/32". Always try sample joints before cutting the wood you intend to use. Run another set of test joints to see if this adjustment has corrected the problem or if further adjustment is needed.

The proper fit has been achieved. The finger joints are snug. The ends of the joints are also flush with the surface of the wood.

Using the same procedures as before, make dado cuts around the bottom edge of the walls of the second coffin.

Shown here, the finger joints and the dado cuts are in place. The dado cuts have been made at the bottom of all four side and end walls. Once assembled, these dados are ready to receive the base.

Now dry fit all 4 side walls. It is perfectly all right to use a piece of scrap wood and a hammer to tap the joints together.

Clamp the end board and glue the block in place. I'm using Hot Stuff instant glue to seal the block and the finger joints. The clamps are so tight normal glue would be squeezed out.

Because of the way the dado was cut for the bottom and the way the finger joints work out, you end up with a void at the bottom that needs to be filled. The best way to fill the void ...

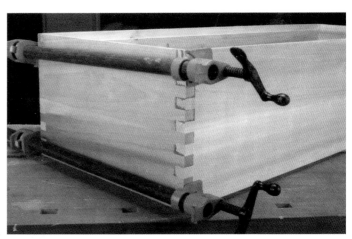

The finger joints are now glued.

... is to cut a small block from the same wood, trying to match the color and grain as closely as possible.

Once the glue is set, the clamps can be removed.

38

Spread yellow carpenter's glue around the inside lip created by the dado cut.

Secure all 8 corners (4 top, 4 bottom) with a dowel that goes through at least 2 of the finger joints. This will prevent the corners from ever spreading under any load. To accomplish this, drill holes into the finger joints with a 3/16" bit set for the proper depth.

Spread the glue out with a brush to get a good seal between the lip and the plywood coffin base. Add 1 1/4" sheet rock screws to keep the base firmly in place.

Tap dowels in place with a small hammer. When firmly seated, cut off the excess wood ...

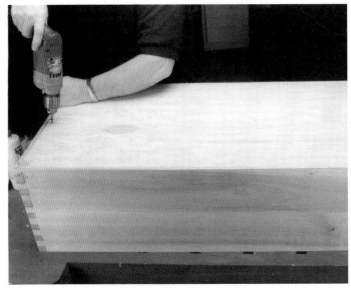

The screws are now in place along the bottom.

... so that the dowel is flush at the surface.

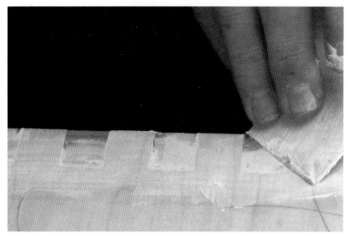

Now fill in all of the voids and imperfections with carpenter's wood filler. Wet the joints a little before filling so that the wood does not pull all of the moisture out of the wood filler.

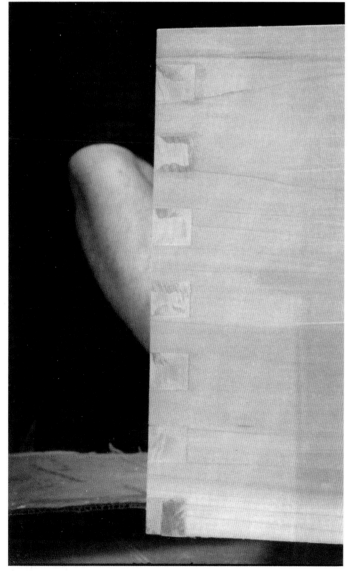

Sand all of the edges and putty smooth.

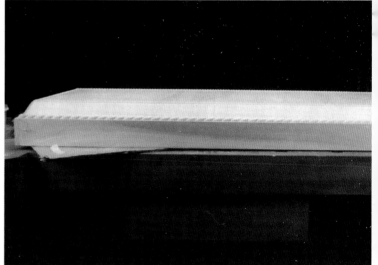

Set aside the base. It is time to construct the top. The two big differences on this lid are: the side band has a 3/8" wide x 1 1/2" deep dado and an extra board has been added in the top to make it slope slightly inward (an optional technique, the board could be set in straight up and down). Refer to the plans for angles needed to construct the sloped side. The construction techniques are the same as those used previously.

The two main types of wood in the lid are poplar (used on the side band and side of the top) and birch plywood ( used on the flat top surface). The rope-like molding and small bead molding are available at most lumber yards. You can also construct your own molding as you will see later.

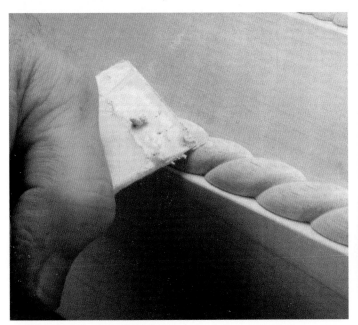

Once the lid is constructed, fill in all holes in the surface with Elmer's Carpenter's Wood Filler.

The corner has been rounded down.

The main problem with this rope-like molding is that it needs hand sculpturing to make a right angle corner.

A little bit of wood putty gives the trimmed down corner a finished look.

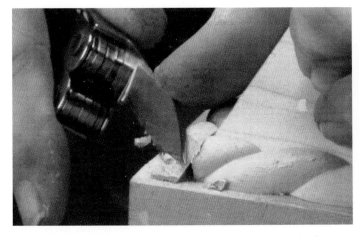

Round down the excess molding with a small knife. Work slowly through this task and the corner will turn out very well.

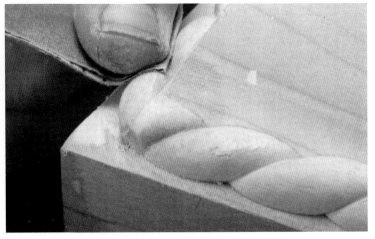

Sand down the putty to finish the corner with 150 grit paper.

Now is a good time to go around and touch up all of the putty work, sanding it smooth. Hand sanding on the molding seems to work better than power sanding. Round all of the corners to give them a little extra chip resistance.

For ease of installation, drill a pilot hole for each of the screws used to secure the leg brackets.

We are going to place legs on this rectangular, poplar finger joint coffin to illustrate that it can be used for another purpose, mainly as a blanket box. It could also be used as some other type of dry storage. The legs are placed 3 1/2" in from the side and end of this very useful box.

Attach the brackets with the screws that came with them. By setting the brackets in 3 1/2", the legs line up with the outer edge of the box and are less likely to trip people.

The brackets for the legs are available at most of your finer hardware or home improvement stores. Place them so that their outer edges are on the 3 1/2" marks on both sides.

The bracket is firmly installed and ready to receive the leg.

Stain the legs using Minwax red mahogany prior to installation.

Install the legs and very carefully turn the box over. Make sure not to knock over your stain when you turn the box over onto its new feet.

Apply the red mahogany stain to the box with a sponge. Use long, smooth strokes to avoid streaking.

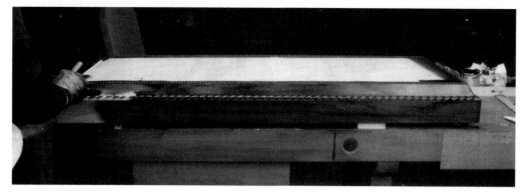

Stain the lid with red mahogany, making sure that all of the crevices in the molding have been filled, creating the proper lights and shadows to make the detail stand out.

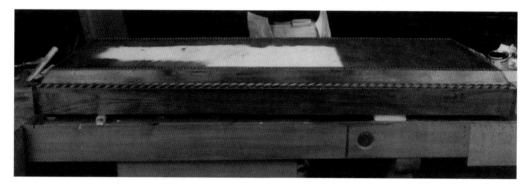

Continue staining the lid using long even strokes to avoid streaking. It is preferable to stroke with the gain as well.

The lid of the box is coated with red mahogany and awaits its final polyurethane varnish. Of course, if this box is to be used inside only two coats of varnish are needed. A minimum of three coats is required for outdoor use.

This multi-purpose box is stained and awaits its final destiny. Coat it with polyurethane varnish before putting it to use.

**The third coffin for people.**

The third coffin is straight sided below the shoulders, tapered inward above the shoulders, made from birch plywood, and finished with half round molding (refer to PLYWOOD COFFIN patterns). Begin construction by cutting all of the birch plywood to the proper width and length as stated in the chart for the birch plywood coffin.

Trim the ends of all of the boards to their proper angles.

Mark all adjacent edges and mark both sides of the joint as guides for the biscuit cutter as shown previously.

Adjust the gauge on the biscuit cutter for number 20 biscuits. Line up the biscuit cutter with all of the witness marks and make all of the cuts for the biscuit joints at once.

The biscuit joints are in place to fit number 20 biscuits. The dado has also been cut into the bottom edge of each board to receive the coffin base.

To make your own molding for the lid of this coffin, run a board (this one is 3/4" thick mahogany) through the shaper. The head in the shaper is a 3/4" bead cutter. Follow the manufacturer's instructions for properly setting up and running this equipment. Be sure to leave all of the guards in place. Carefully run the board through the shaper to get an even, rounded cut.

Cutting the half round molding for the coffin lid is easy and straight-forward on the table saw because the board is flat on the back and the angles can be set on the mitering guide.

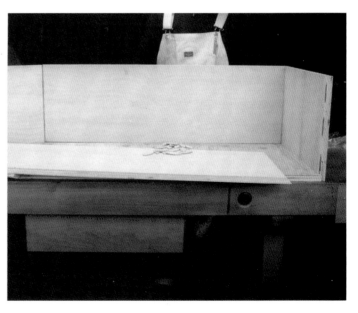

Setting the table saw blade for a straight 3/4" thick cut, separate the bead from the board to form half round molding.

Here we are dry fitting the coffin, using the plywood base as a template.

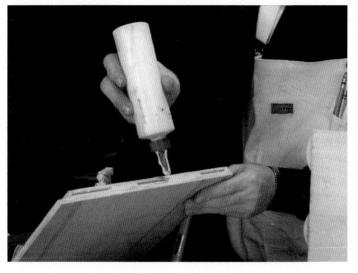

Spread yellow carpenter's glue in a thin, even layer, making sure the glue gets down into the biscuit holes. Remember that these biscuits swell when exposed to glue. Don't wait very long before assembly once biscuits are exposed to glue.

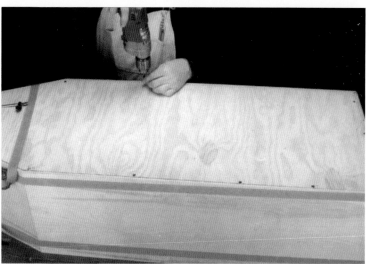

Now would be a good time to fasten the bottom in place. Use yellow carpenter's glue and 1 1/4" long sheet rock screws to secure the base into the dado cut. Set the box aside to dry.

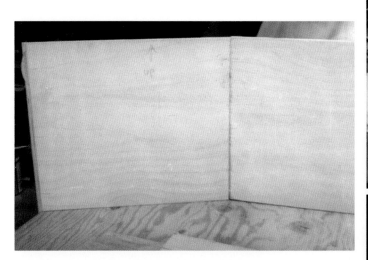

The joint is matched and the biscuits are glued into place.

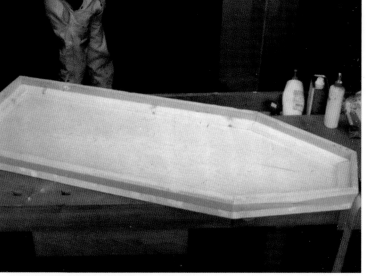

Repeat this assembly process with the lid. Here are the bottom and top views of the assembled lid. The lid is glued, nailed, and all voids are filled with carpenter's putty.

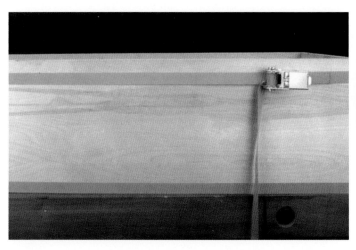

Tighten straps around the coffin, making sure no glue squeezes out underneath the straps. If it does, loosen the straps and clean the glue away. Leave the straps in place until the glue dries.

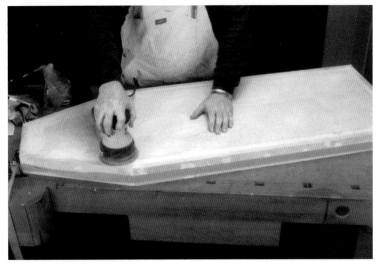

Sand the lid smooth.

Cut and place the half round molding along the top of the lid.

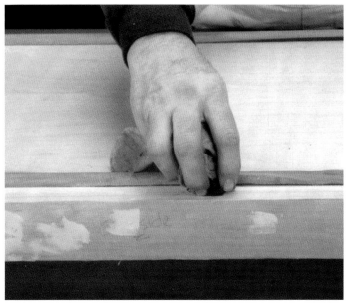

With a damp cloth, wipe off any glue that may have squeezed out from beneath the molding.

Fasten the molding in place with yellow carpenter's glue and brads. Sand the corners where the molding meets to assure an excellent fit.

Apply red mahogany stain to the lid in long strokes to simulate planking.

The lid is stained.

As you apply the red mahogany stain on the coffin body, remember to apply the stain in long strokes to simulate planking. Overlaps are all right because mahogany has color variations.

This birch plywood coffin is finished. The staining is done. It only needs a coat of polyurethane varnish to be complete and ready for action.

**The small pet coffin.**

The small pet coffin is a simple finger jointed box with a flat lid. Follow the pattern and previously discussed techniques to complete the basic box. Apply a wood pressed appliqué to the front of the small pet coffin for a finishing touch. Secure the appliqué with yellow carpenter's glue and small wire brads.

Fill any voids around the finger joints on the small pet coffin with Elmer's Carpenter's Wood Filler.

Using the table saw, make a Kerf cut near to bottom of the side walls to inset the base. Fill the void left when we inset the bottom into the sidewalls. Use a wooden peg cut especially for this purpose and hold it in place with yellow carpenter's glue.

Remove the excess peg with a dove tail saw. Repeat this process on all four corners.

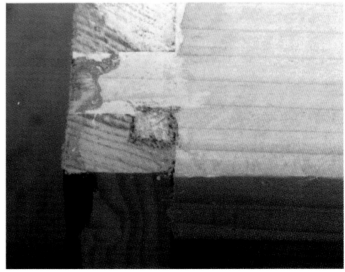

The peg is firmly in place, flush with the outer surface of the coffin.

Sand the coffin smooth.

All parts of the appliqué have been carefully stained.

The small pet coffin is sanded and ready for finish.

The outside of the coffin has been stained. Make sure to wear rubber gloves during this process.

Using red mahogany stain and a sponge, begin staining the small pet coffin. Be very careful to work the stain in well around all parts of the appliqué.

With this mahogany stain, any place that may have had glue on it could well need a second or third coating to cover the glue.

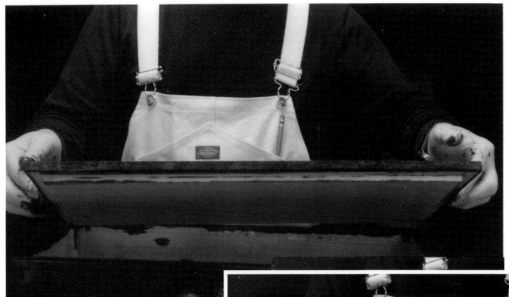

This is a simple, flat lid. It has a 3/4" reveal on the inside so that it fits snugly when put in place. The reveal is made with a dado cut, cut half way into the side of the coffin.

Stain the lid, laying the stain on in long even strokes.

**The medium sized pet coffin**

This is a medium size pet coffin is a simple rectangular box made of pine with half lap corner joints and the bottom inset into a 1/2" dado cut made into all four of the perimeter walls. The half lap is made with a dado cutter set to cut half way through the side wall at each end.

I am using a textured stone finish by Formby to complete this coffin. The color used is granite. I have finished both the inside and outside of the coffin in this color.

The appliqué is adhered to the lid of the box in the same fashion previously described in the book. The lid itself is a flat lid with a 3/4" reveal on the inside.

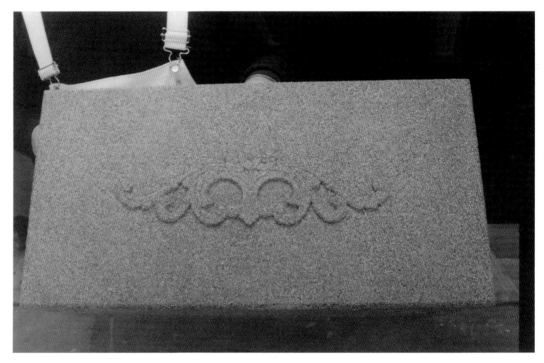

Granite finish is applied over the entire coffin to give it the look of a granite box.

**The large pet coffin.**

This is a large pet coffin made from 3/4" A-A plywood. It has a simple construction, using 90 degree mitered corners held together with glued number 10 biscuits and a bottom that is inset into a dado. The bottom is made from 1/2" thick plywood.

The stain we are applying is a wood stain rubbing oil. It is a rosewood color manufactured by Minwax. Apply this stain with a sponge.

The outside of the large pet coffin is stained.

This stain gives a very good wood grain. It has almost a zebra stripe effect.

The top for the large pet coffin is constructed from 3 different pieces of molding and one piece of 1/2" thick plywood. Two of the moldings are commercially made, a flat frame molding and a piece of cove molding. The third is the half round molding shown manufactured earlier in this book. All of the corners are straight 45 degree corners held together with number 0 biscuits and yellow carpenter's glue. Finishing the inside of this coffin will be left up to your personal preference.

The lid is fully stained. Make sure that you work the stain in around the moldings well so that you leave no white spots.

Details of the inside of the lid.

The completely stained coffin awaiting its final polyurethane gloss coat.

# Gallery